My Life,

My Poems

Erica Washington

My Life, My Poems

Author: Erica Washington
ISBN-13: 978-0692799628
ISBN-10: 0692799621
LCCN: TBD

Editing/Typesetting: Young Dreams Publications T Waller
www.youngdreamsbig.com

Cover Design: POSH ANNOUCEMENTS for YDP

ABOUT THE AUTHOR

I am Erica Washington, an author of poems inspired by many, a mother, which is my greatest gift, and now a fiancé to the best man a woman can ask for. Journey with me and you will see all that I am on pages 1, 2 and 3. I am Erica Washington, enjoy my book and reading about me.❤

Connect with Erica Washington

e.wash26@gmail.com

Instagram: @poetry_is_me2

Acknowledgments

Whether here now,
or gone with the wind,
the **_Love_** & **_Support_** you've given me
will **_Always_** live within.
Thank you.

Dedication

For pushing me
believing in me
for encouraging
& inspiring me to
never give up...
I Dedicate This Book To You

I love Now, I love you Still,
Always have, Always will

Introduction

Here's to love, hurt, inspiration,
happiness and growth.

I've experienced all these
emotions and many more.

Now in my book, *My Life, My Poems*,
you can journey through them with me.

Mirror

There it was, a mirror just for me.

I stood and looked very hard, very long and very careful at this woman wondering who she could be.

She's beautiful, Her eyes bold and brown. Her smile is big, and electrifying.
The best smile around town. A woman of beauty, yes that's she.

But as I looked and looked deeper, I saw her heart and soul.

A heart that is hurt and at times bleeds for affection.

But despite the tears, despite the hurt, there was a heart of gold.

A heart that is pure. It knows no wrong. It's generous.

It loves without hesitation. It's affectionate and very gracious.

A soul that is thoughtful and often forgiving.

So no matter what happens, no matter how she feels or how you feel about her...

She will ALWAYS value and love the her she was meant and made to be. That's her in the mirror.

Yes that is me. As beautiful inside and out as she can be.

Unidentifiable

What if the GREAT that you think you have is not really GREAT at all. It's just better then what you had.

What if the BAD you have is not really BAD at all. It's just not what you want.

What if the RIGHT you have is not really RIGHT at all. It's just all the RIGHT you know.

What if your HAPPIEST moment is not really HAPPY at all? It's just a thought of what could be.

What if you chose to live life and deal with the GREATNESS that happens along the way, accept the BAD things because they will eventually be OK.

Understand your RIGHT to know, really know.

Understand right from wrong and cherish the HAPPIEST moments of your life because they are what makes you strong!

What if...

Love

You know   that feeling where everything   feels right. Where you don't have to worry about tomorrow or yesterday. Where you feel safe knowing you're doing the best you can. The feeling of never being judged. The feeling of being free and knowing you are accepted no matter what. The feeling of never wanting to let go or move forward feeling any other way. The feeling of joy, excitement and relaxation. The feeling of forever and death do us part. Yeah that feeling... It's called love.

Unspoken Words

The fire, the hurt, the anger, the rage, these feelings mind wondering, heart pounding, tears, sadness unspoken words.

Why can't I speak them?
Why can't I tell you what I'm feeling?
Why can't I express to you the emotions that I have.
Who am I hurting?
Do you know I feel this way?

I smile, I laugh, I'm happy, I love and my heart is still open. I have unspoken words, I try to speak them, the thought is there, I form my lips but nothing comes out.

Instead I smile, today is not the day and tomorrow may not work either, but I'm patiently waiting on the moment where my thoughts and emotions become words, that are spoken.

Dear Black Women and Men

In the spirit of Spring.

Take a minute to smile and embrace the CHANGE of seasons.

Nothing stays the same. I am you...

Often, we are so consumed in the right now and
how bad things are RIGHT now.

Remember just like the seasons, nothing stays the same.

Get up today and embrace the CHANGE within YOU.

YOU don't like it, CHANGE it.

It makes YOU unhappy, CHANGE it.

YOU feel YOU have the ability to make it better.

CHANGE it. It all starts with YOU.

SO today I Challenge YOU to embrace your CHANGE.

Loved At The Wrong Time

Love is patient, love is kind, love is also met at the wrong time. When I met you and you met me, the love we shared came instantly, it was greeted with kind words from the heart, it was welcomed with laughter that never stopped. You wanted me as much as I wanted you, nothing made us happier than just us two.

Love is patient, love is kind, love is also met at the wrong time. The love we shared made us both so scared, but we shared it without fear, knowing we will always be there. We shared it freely, freely for the world to see, not knowing people watching wouldn't agree. Anger, rage, and hostility changed the love between you and me. Heart hurting and soul burning knowing the love we shared, the love we had, the love we've known was a love that would no longer be there. I love you, you love me, but we are two souls that aren't meant to be. The love we have, the love we share, isn't enough to stop the careless acts of enemies everywhere.

Love is patient, love is kind, this love was met at the wrong time.

A me...

Who am I?

That was the question.
I knew who I was, when I was with you.
I knew what I wanted and what was shared between us two.
I knew I was her mommy and that was true.
I knew we were a family and needed no proof.
I cooked for you. I cleaned too.
I made my mark on being there for you.
I didn't make a move without first thinking of how it would affect you,
because I knew who I was when I was with you.
But what happens when we stop being a me and a you.

Who am I?
What do I do?
What am I, a me without you?
I need to find me. What will I do?
How will I manage without a me plus you?
 I'm still her mommy and that's still true.
I'll do my best to find a me without you.
God created me without you.

I'll put my faith in Him, and learn to be me, just me not with you.

Please forgive me

I'm thinking of you and these memories are great.

Wishing I had one last conversation,
one last laugh,one last visit to tell you just how much I love you,
just how much my life is not the same without you in it,
and just how much our friendship really means to me.

I've wronged you and for that I'm sorry.

I have not been s great friend to you,

like you've always been to me and that's my mistake.

I've left you with little to no explanation and for that I apologize.

However I've always loved you and
have always held a special place in my heart.

And for that, I say thank you, and ask that you please forgive me.

Judgement Day

Yes I'm here. I'm here to explain. I've done wrong. I haven't been quite right. Some of my choices have been bad and a few more just out of spite. I've hurt people, people that I've loved. I've also made enemies with people sent from up above.

But before you judge me, before you wave the white flag, I have something to say and hopefully you'll understand. My love is pure. My heart is gold. I care very deeply that's what I've been told. So today, I stand before YOU, asking you to please know me, listen to me, and try to appreciate me, before you judge me.

Incomplete

My heart feels empty. My mind has no thoughts. My days are filled with nothing, and my time is wasting away. I'm incomplete. What's missing? Can I get it back? Why am I feeling like this? I have her, him and them. But is that enough? Do they complete ME? I still feel incomplete. Ok, I'm gonna start with me, I have to look deep. My heart knows love. My mind is intact. My thoughts are filled with greatness and for now on, I will spend my days enjoying my happiness, my purpose for life, and my passion with the thought of being and feeling complete.

Lost

Today, I searched and looked I cried out for help, but no one was there.

I was lost. How could this be? Where am I? Why am I by myself?

Feelings of emptiness, sadness and hurt come over me.

I'm alone No escape. Nothing here, and no one to call. I'm so lost.

I hear nothing, just the sound of my heart beating and beating hard.

I'm scared, I'm confused. I no longer wanna be here.

This place, these feelings and these emotions, I'm still lost.

So I sit. I think. I cry. I beg. I walk. I run. I think some more. I'm tired.

I simply can't go on. Today, I chose to do nothing.

No need to worry. No need to cry. No need to beg. No need to whine.

I'll just sit here, alone, with my feelings, my emotions and my thoughts knowing one day they'll find me, and I'll no longer be gone.

SMILE

It's you. It's me.
It's her. It's them.
It's the idea. It's the feel.
It's the love. It's passion.
It's respect. It's conversation.
It's the fear. It's childlike ways.
It's weakness. It's the future.
It's my pride. It's emotion.
It's the days, hour and minutes I've spent living my life...
Yes that's the reason I smile...

Dreamers, Hopers and Believers, too

I'm a dreamer.
A hoper and a believer too.
I'm all of those things, not just one or two.
I live life through dreams, in hopes to one day share.
I love to believe, believing I will always care. I believe that I can.
I believe in one day. I believe in hopes and dreams.
I believe they are here to stay.
But on my quest.
I find this to be true.
Nothing but hopes and dreams, comes to a hoper and a dreamer and a believer too.
Believing will only get you so far on this journey of truth.
With dreaming and hoping and believing too, needs to come DOING, because the doers push through.
The doers are doers.
Not hopers with dreams.
The doers are just doers DOING what they believe.
Today I'll take heed to the doers, stop just hoping and dreaming and I'll start DOING what I believe and what I dream.

No Title

He was working, working hard, I let him in, I must admit, I always did. He came full force, he came so quick, I laid down and couldn't resist. For he came in ways, that I knew was real and nothing could change the way I feel. He came through my child, so tender and mild, but when he did I just broke down. He showed himself through family and friends. Some relationships I thought would never end. One thing after another, one person after person, it hurt like hell, my mind, body and spirit felt I was in jail. My mind was drained. My heart felt weak, often I felt no need to think. For he had me. He had full control. He knew I had no one to talk to. He knew I had no one to call. He knew I had no to even pray for me at all. I was mad, angry and depressed. So I just started talking, talking aloud. No words made sense. No words were off limits. No time to be proud. No time to be afraid. No time to be silent. No time to worry about what to say. Just time to myself. Just time to talk and definitely time to change. Why am I here? No purpose at all. Nothing's worse than continuing to fall. I've reached the end. I couldn't take it anymore. Just when I thought I couldn't say no more, my mind became worthy of words again. My heart beat was different more subtle and steady. Tears flowed down my face and a smile covered my lips. I couldn't control my stomach and its many flips. I had faith, faith in my mind, faith in my God who's been there the whole time. With a simple prayer and a simple try, God came to me, God heard my cry. Now my mind, body and spirit will continue to shine. The devil thought he had me. The devil thought he would win. The devil thought he was becoming my best friend. My God showed up and conquered all. No more being afraid to fall.

Brokenhearted

She found herself. She's open.
Unafraid and ready for life.
But that left her broken hearted. She found her voice.
She spoke up whether right or wrong.
But that left her broken hearted.
She's happy. She smiles more than frowns. She's enjoying life.
She's as happy as can be. But that left her broken hearted.
She's so in love.
Love like she's only imagined, a love she's afraid of losing.
But that left her broken hearted.
She can't go back to what she once was.
Timid, lonely and unhappy. She loves herself.
She loves her voice. She loves her smile.
She loves the love she's in...
but she can't keep feeling broken hearted...
she's so broken hearted.

Without You

The thoughts. The feel. The idea. How can I live?

Where do I go from here? It's been me and you. You and me.

Now that's gone. Tears begin to fall as I think of the good and bad times with you.

The days and nights spent talking, laughing and loving you. Now that's gone.

Will I get it back? Will you come back will you want me back? Will I want you back?

My mind is wondering, racing. My head hurting.

These thoughts, these thoughts of me and you, the thoughts of you and me consumes me.

I don't know when the pain will leave or how long I will hurt.

But I know that I love you, and I always will.

If I have to live without you, I hope the thoughts of me and you, continue to live within you.

My Prayer

I've prayed for you more often than I've prayed for myself.

I've loved you more often than I've loved myself. I've given you more of me than I've given anyone else.

I taught you how to love, in hopes that you would give me the love that I needed, no matter the good, bad or hard times.

As I look around and see how the days, hours and minutes have so drastically changed.

I realize, I can only pray so much, love so much, and give so much until there's nothing left.

I will always love you. That's a fact. But I have to let you go, in hopes one day you'll come back.

To pray for me as much, love me as much, and give me as much as I've given you!

Overwhelmed

Nights,
days,
hours and minutes I cry,
my time is limited.
I'm overwhelmed.

My funds are low.
I'm overwhelmed.
My mind is crowded.
I'm overwhelmed.

I work,
I cook,
I clean,
but my mind is still overwhelmed!

What do I do?
Who do I call?
How do I process these thoughts and still go on?

These thoughts.
My funds.
My time and my life.
I must maintain... to say the least I won't complain.

Lust

I meet it, knowing it has been great!
I feel it. I truly hold it tight.
I talk to it. Conversations that only I can have.
They last forever. Never a silent moment.
It's my friend. Deep down, and to the end.
I taste it. Nothings ever tasted sweeter.
Its patient and kind. Most of the time.
It has its moments where nothing is right, but in that moment it never leaves my side.
It's great.
It's amazing, and just plain dynamite.
Love is what it is.
I hope you're lucky enough to find it, because lust just won't do.

Believe

I believe in you. I believe in me.
I believe in a world where we can be free.
I believe in unicorns, they're white and fly too, I believe that, don't you?
I believe in planets and that the earth is blue.
I believe in the sun and the moon too.
I believe in love and I believe in pain.
I believe in moments that become memories with little to no gain.
I believe in you and I believe in me.
I believe that we are meant to be.
Believing is not just seeing.
Believing is feeling too.
That one day those feelings will get you through.
Heartaches and pain, stress and strain.
I believe, that I can believe, which will one day set me free.
The power to believe….

Me

Today I am me. I am the only me I see. Yesterday, I was me. I was the only me I wanted to be. Tomorrow I'll be me. I'll be the only me that stands as tall as a tree. I want to be me. I love being me. My heart desires and strives to be a greater me. So before you judge or ridicule me, before you suggest me being someone other than me, before you violate or even disrespect me, try to understand me, for simply being me, because that's all I'll ever be, is plain ole me.

Sista, My Sista

Girl don't you cry.
Don't you moan.
Don't you weep, because you can move mountains if you just stop to think.

Girl don't be sad or let worrying get to you, because half the battle is won and the hard part is almost through.

Girl don't you mope or say you're depressed.
Life's not done and you have yet to see the rest.

Girl don't go running around saying you're mad.
The brain is more powerful than anything said.

So girl fix your face and your attitude too, that's what they want for you to do.

Simply stop so they can stick a label on you.

Girl you are beautiful, bold and brilliant and you my sista are very resilient.

Girl take your time, stand nice and tall, for you are standing, not just for you but girl for us all.

Alone

It's quiet, I'm alone. No one to talk to. No one to hold or keep me company. I'm alone. TV is on, but it's not what I want. I'm still alone. My mind starts to wonder, these thoughts become intense. The thoughts of you and me, me and you. I laugh and smile, then I look around, only to find, I'm still alone. I feel you, feels as if you're here with me. Our conversations are lasting, your touch so soft, and your presence I love. Meanwhile, I turn over to your side of the bed and I'm still alone. Grab your pillow, take a deep breath, your scent I smell and a smile comes across my face. Why am I smiling? Why do I feel so happy I wonder?! I lay here knowing I'm alone, but with the thoughts of you and me, me and you, I'm never lonely.

Dear Love

Why me? Why now? Why him? I can't explain the joy, happiness and confusion I feel. I wonder and second guess you as often as I breathe. Did you come for me? Am I supposed to be this happy? But no one is happy for me.

Why? It hurts, it breaks me down. It also makes me cry. You're supposed to be the happiness that completes me, the strength I need and the piece of the puzzle that is missing.

Ok, so it's up to me. The time is now. The feeling is great and I'm ready. I'm enjoying the ride. I smile more than I frown and I have more faith in you than I could have ever imagined.

You're here. You came for me. You brought me intimacy, tenderness, endearment, excitement... You brought me love, so I breathe, I accept and I love you back... and for that I thank you!

Oh this bed

I came upstairs and laid in the bed, oh this bed, it's where I lay holding you, where I often said I love you and where we've made love too.

I held the pillow, closed my eyes took one dep breath and to my surprise, the tears started flowing right out of my eyes. I haven't been able to control these thoughts and emotions too.

The idea of never being able to lay in this bed again with you. Bae, I love you, I'm in love too and simply can't imagine living life without you. I smile at our ups and frown at our downs, wondering why we we're having more frowns than smiles. No matter the answer. No matter the truth, I simply can't imagine life without you.

So I'll stay in this bed and hold this pillow, hoping to one day stay in this bed holding you. Oh this bed.

Dear Yesterday

You are very different than today. But you have the same similarities as the day before yesterday. What I experienced from today was joy, peace, love and an abundance of warmth and happiness. I received it from him, her and them.

However did I actually receive it. Or, did I just know in my heart it was there? Now yesterday the experience were distant, a little uneasy at times, but still very warm and loving. But was it really distant and uneasy? Or, did I make myself feel that way because it was in fact different from today?

But the day before yesterday him, her and them showered the love, made me feel special and wanted. I enjoyed it. I loved it, I wanted it and some part of my heart needed it. It was there. It was something that came from the heart with little to no direction.

With yesterday, today and the day before yesterday... I learned everyday is not going to be the same. However, the love, the feelings and joy that him, her and them bring will ALWAYS remain the same in my heart. Those feelings of warmth will ALWAYS be with me and that happiness will ALWAYS put a smile on my face in my darkest hour.

Thank you today, yesterday and the day before yesterday, You've given me reasons to move on. And now, I'm looking forward to tomorrow. I love already.

Him

He told me he loved me, He told me I was beautiful.
He made me smile. He tried to arouse me with his words.
He tried to capture my soul.
He found me attractive, No matter what I wore,
He gazed in my eyes, this time, like never before.
His thoughts of me so genuine and true.
He just couldn't help it, he needed to tell me,
just how amazing of a woman I am.
How I speak with so much passion
and just how sexy he sees me.
I heard it, I listen, I acknowledge it.
Why aren't I happy? Why don't I care?
Why can't I appreciate how he feels?
I know now, I understand and I accept that
he just isn't him.

Moving on

This is hard.

Harder than I thought. The thoughts of moving on, moving forward and moving right out of your life. The weeks, days and hours leading up to this were the worse. I cried many times. I've had sleepless nights.

How can I move on? What am I to do?

With the thought of knowing I'm moving right on from you. This can't be. This really isn't true, I'm not emotionally, physically or mentally ready to move on from you.

My mind is racing. My heart ponding. I pick up the phone to make one last call to you.

No answer.

Thinking to myself, you know just what you have to do, because he has already moved right on, right on from you.

Questions

Why did I do that?
What was I thinking?
Did that help me?
What do I do now?
Why me?
Did I make the right choice?
What was I thinking?
Is now the time?
When should I do that?
Why me?
What was I thinking?
Where do I go from here?
Was that the right move?
Is that meant for me?
What was I thinking?
Who can I count on?
Why me?
Wait, why not me?

What's meant for me, I will not have to question.

Hurt

He hurt me, but I still love.

She hurt me, but I still love.

It hurt me, but I still love.

Tears, heartache, sorrow, guilt, rage and desire to understand the hurt. Excitement, happiness, passion, patience and vulnerability to love again. To know it, to have felt it, and truly understand the power of love is to never go back to being hurt again.

Although I've been hurt, I will always love.

Cayla-Nicole

AS I LOOK OUT THE WINDOW AND GAZE DOWN AT THE GROUND, I THINK ABOUT HOW I WANT TO MAKE YOU PROUD. I'M A HARD WORKING MOTHER, WHAT I'VE ALWAYS DREAMT I'LL BE, DOING THE BEST JOB I CAN FOR YOU AND ME. IT DOES GET HARD, I WON'T LIE AND SAY IT DON'T, BUT TO THINK OF GIVING UP, NO SORRY, I JUST WON'T. I'LL MAKE YOU PROUD, UPSET AND ANGRY TOO, THAT'S MY JOB, BUT YOU'LL ALWAYS FORGIVE ME, EVEN FOR THE HURTFUL THINGS I DO. I'M YOUR MOMMY, I STAND STRONG, TALL AND BRAVE, IT'S NOT ALWAYS EASY, BUT I WOULDN'T HAVE IT ANY OTHER WAY. WE SHARE THIS BOND, IT'S AMAZING I THINK, TWO SOULS TRYING TO FIGURE OUT LIFE AND BE AS HAPPY AS CAN BE. WE WILL RUN INTO OBSTACLES WHERE THAT BOND WILL BE TESTED, I'M SURE IT WILL HAPPEN MORE OFTEN THAN EXPECTED, DON'T FREAK OUT, DON'T WORRY OR RUN, UNDERSTAND THAT IT'S SO MUCH BETTER ONCE THE BATTLE IS WON. I LOVE YOU MORE THAN YOU'LL EVER KNOW, I'LL WALK ON WATER, THROUGH HOT COALS OR EVEN BARE FEET IN THE SNOW, JUST TO GET TO YOU, TO CARRY YOU, PROTECT YOU, GUIDE YOU, TO HUG YOU AND NEVER LET YOU GO. I'M YOUR MOMMY AND THAT'S ALL YOU'LL EVER NEED TO KNOW.

Unspoken Words Part 2

Heart racing. No words to be spoken. Tears flowing.
No words to be spoken. Head hurting. No words to be spoken.
No words to be spoken.

But there are words to be spoken. Mind racing. No words to be spoken.
Legs shaking. No words to be spoken. No words to be spoken,
but there are words to be spoken.

Hands shaking. No words to be spoken. No words to be spoken,
but there are words to be spoken. I've gotten here again,
where my words are unspoken, I know what to
say, I know how to feel.

I know what I want, but I can't seal the deal. I can't speak the words
that are left unspoken. I can't speak the words. I can't change
the feel. Can't imagine living this life with these
words that are here.

My mind is still racing.
The tears are still flowing,
but I still can't speak these words
that are sadly left unspoken.

The Beginning...

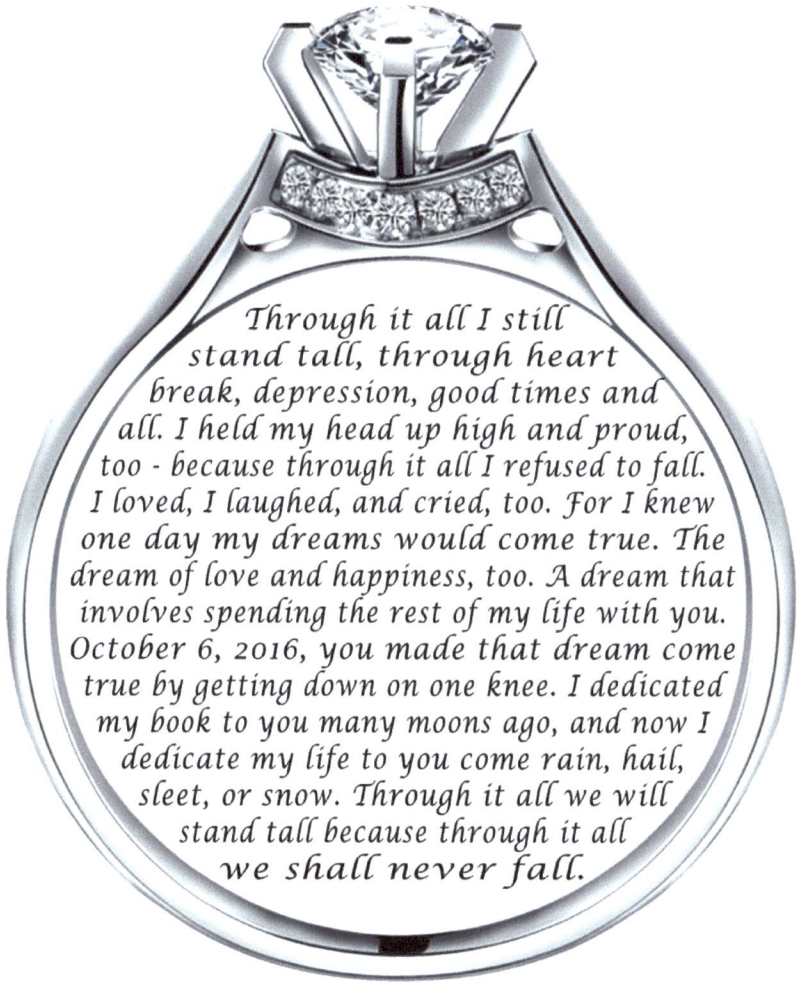

Through it all I still stand tall, through heart break, depression, good times and all. I held my head up high and proud, too - because through it all I refused to fall. I loved, I laughed, and cried, too. For I knew one day my dreams would come true. The dream of love and happiness, too. A dream that involves spending the rest of my life with you. October 6, 2016, you made that dream come true by getting down on one knee. I dedicated my book to you many moons ago, and now I dedicate my life to you come rain, hail, sleet, or snow. Through it all we will stand tall because through it all we shall never fall.

www.ingramcontent.com/pod-product-compliance
Lightning Source LLC
Chambersburg PA
CBHW041759040426
42447CB00001B/19